ISBN: 9798419266179

Imprint: Independently published

Disclaimer: All answers are correct as of 16th March 2022.

Welcome to

THE
FOOTBALL
QUIZ BOOK

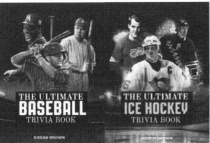

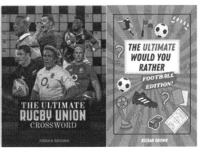

CHECK OUT OUR OTHER PUZZLE BOOKS ON THE WORLD'S
BIGGEST SPORTS. AVAILABLE NOW ON AMAZON.

CONTENTS PAGE

"Football is played with the head. Your feet are just the tools"

- Andrea Pirlo

"When I score I don't celebrate. It's my job, does a postman celebrate when he delivers the post?"

- Mario Balotelli

"My wife doesn't like football. One day she called me 10 minutes before a game to ask where I was"

- Peter Crouch

"To put it in gentleman's terms, if you've been out for a night and you're looking for a young lady and you pull one, you've done what you set out to do. We didn't look our best today but we pulled. Some weeks the lady is good looking and some weeks she's not. Our performance today would have been not the best looking bird but at least we got her in the taxi. She may not have been the best looking lady we ended up taking home but it was still very pleasant and very nice, so thanks very much and let's have coffee."

- Ian Holloway

Warm-Up

Some nice easy questions to get you warmed up!

1. What nationality is Lionel Messi?

2. Who won the 2018 FIFA World Cup?

3. What colour boots do referees traditionally have to wear?

4. What Premier League club do the Glazer family own?

5. What club has Robert Lewandowski scored over 300 goals for?

6. Who are Everton's city rivals?

7. Which player made a world-record move from Barcelona to PSG for €222m in 2017?

8. Who won the 2020/21 Premier League title?

9. What legendary Dutch player has a famous turn named after him?

10. What country are Benfica from?

1. Which club has gone the longest at the start of a season without winning a game (17 matches)?

2. The first-ever goalkeeper to score in the Premier League was Peter Schmeichel. Which club was he playing for?

3. Who is the all-time top goal scorer in the Premier League?

4. Which Premier League team plays at St Mary's Stadium?

5. Name three of the six Premier League teams that have never been relegated.

6. Which manager led Brentford to their first Premier League promotion?

7. Who became manager of Manchester United after Sir Alex Ferguson?

8. What number did Eric Cantona wear for Manchester United?

9. Which player has won the most Golden Boots?

10. Who was in goal for the infamous 'beach ball goal' in a 2009 game between Sunderland and Liverpool?

11. What minute of stoppage time did Sergio Agüero score his title-winning goal against QPR in 2012?

12. Who did Luis Suarez bite against Chelsea in 2012?

13. Which player has the most yellow cards in the Premier League ever?

14. Which club holds the record for the longest run of matches without receiving a red card (107 matches)?

15. What year did the first Premier League season begin?

16. Which club has the most Premier League losses of all-time?

17. Who is the youngest Premier League goal-scorer at 16 years and 270 days old?

18. Who has scored the fastest hat-trick in the Premier League (2 minutes 56 seconds)?

19. How many teams were in the Premier League in its inaugural season?

20. What is the highest-scoring game in Premier League history?

1. Who is La Liga's top scorer of all time with 474 goals?

2. Which team has won the fourth-most La Liga titles with 8?

3. Who are Sevilla's city rivals?

4. Which Argentinian side did Diego Simeone manage before taking the Atlético Madrid job?

5. Which team won their first and only La Liga title in 2000?

6. Which club has come runners-up in La Liga the most times?

7. Who are Valencia's city rivals?

8. Barcelona, Real Madrid and what other club has never been relegated?

9. What La Liga team did David Silva join from Manchester City?

10. What decade was La Liga founded? 1920s, 30s, 40s or 50s?

11. Why was La Liga suspended from 1937 to 1939?

12. How many clubs have won La Liga?

13. What is the highest number of goals that Cristiano Ronaldo scored in a La Liga season? 36, 40, 44 or 48?

14. Which manager won two league titles and a UEFA Cup with Valencia in the early 2000s?

15. What is the match between Real Madrid and Barcelona called?

16. Who has the most La Liga appearances of all time?

17. Who is the highest scoring Frenchman in La Liga?

18. Which Real Betis player, active as of the 2021/22 season, is second on the all-time league appearance list?

19. Which striker scored 228 goals in 550 games for Real Madrid between 1994 and 2010?

20. How many golden boots has Lionel Messi won?

1. Which club has won the most Serie A titles?

2. Who is the Serie A top goalscorer?

3. Who has the most appearances in Serie A?

4. What is Juventus' club nickname?

5. When was Serie A founded? 1898, 1938, 1978 or 2008?

6. What is the official name of the stadium shared by Inter Milan and AC Milan?

7. How many Serie A titles did Paolo Maldini win?

8. What are the two primary colours of Sassuolo?

9. Which team has won the fourth-most titles with 6?

10. Sampdoria is based in which city?

11. What is the name of the Italian domestic cup?

12. Which club, playing in Serie A since 2016, are based on the island of Sardinia?

13. Which South American nation's top division is also called Serie A?

14. Who is Juventus's all-time top goalscorer?

15. Who was the manager of Lazio when they won their last Serie A title in 2000?

16. Which side won five titles in a row in the 2000s?

17. What does Scudetto mean?

18. In what season did Francesco Totti win his sole Serie A title?

19. Which Englishman joined AC Milan from Chelsea in 2021?

20. Who made a €70m move to Juventus from Fiorentina in 2022?

1. Who is the Bundesliga all-time top goalscorer?

2. When was the Bundesliga founded? 1963, 1973, 1983 or 1993?

3. Which team has won the joint-second number of titles alongside Borussia Dortmund with five?

4. Which team has played the most seasons in the Bundesliga?

5. How many teams from West Berlin were in the inaugural Bundesliga season? 0, 1, 2 or 3?

6. Which Eintracht Frankfurt one-club man holds the record for most Bundesliga appearances with 602?

7. How many games does each team play a season?

8. Who were the last team other than Bayern Munich or Dortmund to win the league?

9. Which side, led by talisman Mario Gomez, won the 2006/07 title?

10. Which club, nicknamed 'The Billy Goats' were the inaugural winners of the Bundesliga?

11. Which Peruvian striker is the top-scoring non-European in the Bundesliga with 197 goals?

12. Which side, competing in the 2021/22 season, is based in East Berlin?

13. How many league titles does a team need to win to be able to wear a star above their badge?

14. When was the last time Borussia Dortmund won the Bundesliga?

15. Which team has finished second the most times without winning the title (seven)?

16. What does Bundesliga mean in English?

17. What does the word Bayern mean?

18. What Norweigian striker scored a hat-trick on his Bundesliga debut off the bench in 2020?

19. What was the transfer fee paid to Borussia Dortmund by Bayern Munich for Robert Lewandowski in 2014?

20. What does BVB on the Dortmund badge stand for?

1. Which team won the 2020/21 Ligue 1 title?

2. Which team has won the most Ligue 1 titles with 10?

3. Which French side were European Cup runners up in 1956 and 1959?

4. Which Englishman became a cult hero after a short spell at Marseille for the 2012/13 season?

5. What year was PSG founded? 1940, 1950, 1960 or 1970?

6. What season did Marseille win their last title?

7. In what year did the league change its name from Division 1 to Ligue 1? 2000, 2002, 2004 or 2006?

8. What number did David Beckham wear at PSG?

9. Who has been the official sponsor of Ligue 1 since 2020?

10. Which side, inspired by Olivier Giroud's 21 league goals, won their first Ligue 1 title in 2012?

11. Who is PSG's top goalscorer?

12. Who are the only non-French team to play in Ligue 1?

13. Who is the record scorer in Ligue 1 with 299 goals in the 70s and 80s?

14. What was the score when Lyon hosted Marseille in November 2009? 4-4, 4-5, 5-5 or 6-5?

15. Which Marseille player won the Ballon d'Or in 1991?

16. Which player has made the most Ligue 1 appearances with 618?

17. Which team won all seven of their titles consecutively?

18. What is the Ligue 1 trophy called?

19. Which team, nicknamed La Maison Jaune (The Yellow House), won Ligue 1 in 2001?

20. How many clubs have played in Ligue 1? 64, 74, 84 or 94?

1. Which team has won the most Liga Portugal titles?

2. Which Russian team was famous for signing Samuel Eto'o and Roberto Carlos?

3. Which Porto based team won the Primeira Liga in 2001?

4. Which former Liverpool and France striker won back-to-back Greek Superliga golden boots with Panathinaikos in 2010 and 2011?

5. Who has won the most Süper Lig titles?

6. Which team has won the most Greek league titles?

7. Which Danish team won their 11th title in 2021?

8. What is the Belgian league called?

9. Despite playing in the Swiss leagues, what microstate are Vaduz from?

10. How many teams are in the Belgian league and Eredivisie?

11. Which side's name was intended to mimic that of the Basel-based club Old Boys?

12. Which two teams play in Serbia's eternal derby?

13. Who has won the most Eredivisie titles?

14. Who are Dinamo Zagreb's eternal rivals?

15. Which 13-times champions of Ukraine were forced to relocate from the war-torn Donbas region to another part of the country in 2014?

16. Who has won the most Russian league titles with 10?

17. Which Bulgarian shared the 1989/90 European Golden Shoe?

18. What Ukrainian city is Metalist based in?

19. Who has won the most Swiss Super League titles?

20. Who is the Süper Lig's all-time leading goalscorer with 249 goals?

1. What does MVP stand for?

2. What former Juventus, Inter, Milan, Barcelona, PSG and Manchester United striker signed for LA Galaxy in 2018?

3. How many teams are in the MLS as of 2022?

4. In what year did Wayne Rooney join D.C United?

5. Who is the MLS all-time assist leader?

6. Which team has won the most MLS cups?

7. How many Canadian teams are in the MLS?

8. What player did LA Galaxy sign from Real Madrid in 2007?

9. Who has scored the most goals in a single MLS season with 34?

10. What trophy is awarded for the most regular-season points?

11. Who won the 2021 MLS Cup?

12. What MLS club does David Beckham own?

13. Which MLS team did Thierry Henry play for?

14. Who has scored the most hat-tricks in MLS history?

15. Which team plays at Pizza Hut Park?

16. Which team is based in the province of British Colombia?

17. The Red Patch Boys are supporters of what team?

18. What year was the first MLS season?

19. What MLS team is based in Northern California?

20. Which city's team used to be known as the Impact?

1. Which team has won the most Champions League titles with 13?

2. Who is the Champions League's top goalscorer?

3. Of the top 10 scorers in European Cup/Champions League history, which Argentinian has the best goal ratio with 0.84?
(Clue: it's not Lionel Messi)

4. Which player scored a hat-trick against Ajax in the 2019 Champions League semi-final second leg?

5. What year was the European Cup renamed as the Champions League?
1986, 1988, 1990 or 1992?

6. Who is the only player to win three Champions Leagues with three different teams?

7. Who holds the record for most assists in a single Champions League season with 9 in the 2017/18 season?

8. How many teams are in the group stage of the Champions League?

9. Which city did Liverpool stage their 2005 comeback over AC Milan?

10. How many English clubs have won the competition since its inception?

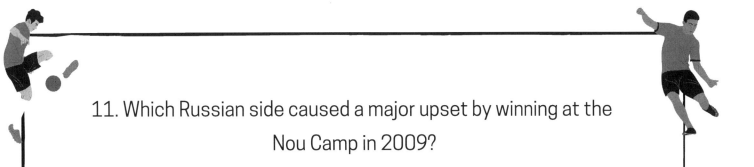

11. Which Russian side caused a major upset by winning at the Nou Camp in 2009?

12. Which club has the most Champions League final losses?

13. Name two of the three UEFA member island countries that have never had a club make the Champions League group stage.

14. How many Champions League titles have PSG won?

15. Which team have lost the most finals without winning the trophy?

16. Which Hungarian scored 4 goals in the 1960 European Cup Final?

17. Which team has won the Champions League more times than their domestic league?

18. How many teams have won the Champions League? 16, 22, 28 or 34?

19. Which former Champions League winning team holds the record for most defeats in the competition?

20. Which Frenchman has missed the most Champions League penalties with 5?

1. Who has won the most Europa Leagues?

2. How many teams are in the Europa League first knockout stage?

3. Which placed Premier League team, receives Europa League group stage qualification?

4. How many Europa League trophies as Unai Emery won?

5. Who won the 2020/21 Europa League final?

6. Three of the four 2011 Semi-final sides were from which country?

7. Which Spaniard has won the most Europa League titles with five?

8. Which club lost consecutive finals in 2013 and 2014?

9. Which Belgian club holds the record for most consecutive appearances in the UEFA Cup and Europa League with 20?

10. Who are the only Turkish team to win the competition?

11. Who were the last two teams from the same country in a Europa League final?

12. Who is the all-time leading Europa League goalscorer?

13. What city was the 2019 Europa League final held in?

14. Whom did Manchester United beat in the 2017 Final?

15. How many times has Real Madrid won the UEFA Cup/Europa League?
0, 1, 2 or 3 times?

16. Which striker, nicknamed 'El Tigre', holds the record for most goals in a
single campaign with 17?

17. The first-ever final featuring two teams from the same nation came in
1972 when Spurs beat what Midlands team?

18. In the 1990s, four of the ten finals featured an all what final?
English, German, Italian or Spanish?

19. Which Italian side won the UEFA Cup in 1994 despite finishing 13th in
Serie A?

20. Which Russian club came from a 4-0 first leg deficit to win 8-5 on
aggregate (AET) in the 2018/19 Third qualifying round against
Dynamo Minsk?

1. How many teams are in the Football League?

2. Which team, nicknamed 'The Cobblers' won League 2 with a record of 99 points in 2016?

3. Occurring in four matches, what is the record for most red cards in a game?

4. How many teams get promoted from League 2?

5. How many play-off places are in each league?

6. Which striker is the only player to win back-to-back Championship golden boots, doing so in 2008 and 2009?

7. What animal is on the Hull City badge?

8. One of the last Championship players to win a cap, which striker was also the first and only Cardiff City player to win an England cap?

9. Who was the official sponsor of the Football League from 2004-2010?

10. Which team has the record for most points in a season (3 points for a win – 46 matches) with 106?

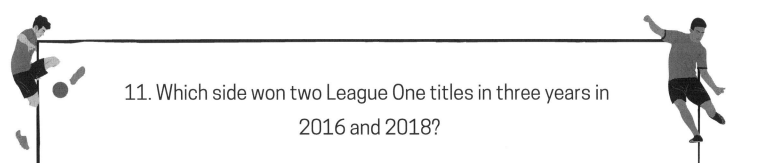

11. Which side won two League One titles in three years in 2016 and 2018?

12. Which team won the 1989/90 Second Division (Championship) play-off final but were not promoted due to financial irregularities?

13. Since 2018, which TV Channel has shown the Football League highlights?

14. What is the biggest stadium in League One in the 2021/22 season?

15. In what year was the second tier renamed as the 'Championship'?

16. When was the Football League founded? 1868, 1878, 1888 or 1898?

17. Name one of three clubs that have won all four divisions in English football.

18. What team are nicknamed 'The Pilgrims'?

19. How many league games do teams play in a season?

20. Who, in 2022, broke the record for most goals in the Championship of all-time?

1. Which team has won the most FA Cups with 14?

2. What was the League Cup called between 2003 and 2014?

3. In 1988, who became the first goalkeeper to save a penalty in an FA Cup Final?

4. When was the first League Cup held? 1960, 1965, 1970 or 1975?

5. What decade was the first FA Cup held?

6. Which individual player has won the most FA Cups?

7. In what year were Category One academy sides added to the EFL Trophy? 2016, 2017, 2018 or 2019?

8. Which player has the most goals in FA Cup finals with 5?

9. How much does a club earn for winning the League Cup? £10k, £100k, £1m or £10m?

10. Who were the last team outside the top division to win the FA Cup?

11. Which club won four League Cups in a row between 2018 and 2021?

12. Who has scored in the most FA Cup Finals?

13. Who is the one non-English team to win the FA Cup?

14. Which National League side won away at a Premier League side in the 2016/2017 FA Cup?

15. Who controversially refused to be subbed in the 2019 Carabao Cup Final and missed the crucial penalty in the 2022 Final?

16. Name one of the two players to win the League Cup a record six times.

17. What is the biggest League Cup aggregate win in a semi-final coming when Man City beat Burton Albion in 2019?

18. Which Midlands club are the only side to win multiple League Cups without losing a final?

19. Who was the last club to win the FA Cup for the first time?

20. Nicknamed 'The Robins', who are the most successful club in what is now called the EFL Trophy with three titles?

1. Who is the UEFA Super Cup held between?

2. Who won the 2021/22 Super Cup?

3. Which English club has won the most Super Cups with three titles?

4. Name one of the two clubs that have won the most Super Cups?

5. Which stadium hosted the Super Cup from 1998-2012?

6. Which club has won the Super Cup three times without winning the Champions League?

7. Who scored a first-half hat-trick in the 2012 Super Cup against Chelsea?

8. Which UK stadium hosted the 2021 Super Cup?

9. What year was the Cup Winner's Cup abolished? 1995, 1997, 1999 or 2001?

10. What country will the inaugural Conference League Final be held in? Albania, Armenia, Austria or Azerbaijan?

11. Which Italian side were the final ever winners of the UEFA Cup Winners' Cup?

12. Who was Aberdeen manager when they beat Real Madrid in the 1983 Cup Winners' Cup Final?

13. Who were the only team from the Soviet Union to win multiple Cup Winners' Cup titles (two)?
Dynamo Dresden, Dynamo Kiev, Dynamo Moscow or Dinamo Tbilisi?

14. Which Scottish side featured in the first-ever Cup Winners' Cup Final in 1961?

15. Which English stadium hosted the final ever European Cup Winners' Cup Final? Anfield, Highbury, St James' Park or Villa Park?

16. Which player scored a last-minute goal with a 40-yard lob over David Seaman, securing the win for Real Zaragoza in the 1995 Cup Winners' Cup Final?

17. What season did the first UEFA Conference League take place?

18. What year was the Intertoto Cup abolished?

19. Which English side were the outright winners of the 2006 Intertoto Cup? Bolton, Everton, Newcastle or West Ham?

20. Which Norweigian side beat Jose Mourinho's Roma 6-1 in the inaugural Conference League?

1. What is the nickname of the derby between Celtic and Rangers?

2. Which team won five out of six Irish league titles between 2014 and 2019?

3. Who are the one team from Northern Ireland who plays in the League of Ireland?

4. What does SPFL stand for?

5. How many teams are in Wales' top division and the SPFL?

6. Which university side featured in the 2019/20 Europa League qualifying?

7. Who is the most successful club in the SPFL?

8. Who were the last team other than Celtic or Rangers to win the Scottish league?

9. Name one of the 'Big Two' in the Northern Irish league.

10. Name one of the two teams to have never been relegated from Ireland's top flight.

11. How many teams are in the League of Ireland?

12. When was the SPFL formed? 1890, 1910, 1930 or 1950?

13. Who are the oldest team in Scotland?

14. Which side who won three successive promotions between 2005 and 2007, reached the Scottish Cup Final and the UEFA Cup qualifying rounds in 2006 before dissolving in 2008.

15. What is the name of Hibernian's stadium?

16. Who scored the most SPFL goals of all-time?

17. Which Scottish side played at Love Street from 1894-2009?

18. What is the most goals in a single SPFL game?

19. Based in England, which team has won the Welsh League the most times?

20. Which Welshman was Europe's highest scorer in the 2000/01 season with 47 league goals and is the all-time leading goalscorer in the Cymru Premier with 319?

1. Who were the winners of the 2019/20 Premier League title?

2. Which goalkeeper has the most clean sheets in Premier League history?

3. Who has the most assists in Premier League history?

4. At what stadium did Blackburn Rovers win the 1994/95 league title on the final day?

5. What season did Leicester City win the Premier League?

6. Who is the only player to have lost two Premier League games in which he has scored a hat-trick (losing both games 4-3)?

7. Who was the Premier League's first £100m signing?

8. Where do Burnley play their home matches?

9. Who plays their home matches at Selhurst Park?

10. The last all-English XI (Aston Villa) and first-ever all-foreign first XI (Chelsea) took place in what year?

11. Who has recorded the fewest points in a Premier League season with 11?

12. Who has scored the most goals in a single 38-game Premier League season (32)?

13. Which Tottenham player was top scorer in the first Premier League season?

14. Which club only picked four non-British players in its time in the Premier League? Barnsley, Coventry, Hull or Oldham?

15. Who is the highest scoring non-English player in the Premier League?

16. Which player has scored the most Premier League own goals?

17. Who is the bottom team in an all-time Premier League table?

18. Which player has been caught offside the most times in Premier League history?

19. Who is the most subbed player in Premier League history (134)?

20. Who scored the first Premier League goal?

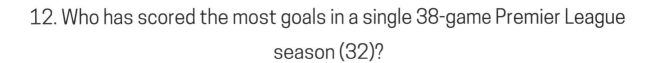

1. Who is the most expensive La Liga transfer of all-time?

2. Who has been president of La Liga since 2013?

3. Since 2016, which bank has sponsored La Liga?

4. Who is the only African player to win the La Liga golden boot?

5. Other than Barcelona, which La Liga club did Diego Maradona play for?

6. Which English manager led Barcelona to the 1984 league title, their first in ten years?

7. Which La Liga stadium has the biggest capacity?

8. What city is Espanyol located in?

9. What is the most amount of teams that have played in a La Liga season? 20, 22, 24 or 26?

10. How many La Liga titles have Sevilla won? 1, 3, 5 or 7?

11. When were Atletico Madrid last in the second division?

12. How many seasons did Cristiano Ronaldo play in La Liga?

13. Which Mexican striker scored 234 La Liga goals for Atletico Madrid, Real Madrid and Rayo Vallecano?

14. To the nearest 5,000, what is the Mestalla's capacity?

15. Rayo Vallecano and Getafe are based in which city?

16. Which Dutchman was the first player to join a Spanish side for a world record fee?

17. What goalkeeper has kept the most clean sheets in La Liga history?

18. How many teams get relegated from La Liga each season?

19. Which side is based in Pamplona?

20. Which two-time Real Madrid president was the first and sole chairman of the breakaway European Super League?

1. What does the 'AC' in AC Milan stand for?

2. Which striker joined Inter Milan for a world record fee of €49m in 1999?

3. What Italian club did Graeme Souness play for in the 1980s?

4. How many Serie A titles have AC Milan won? 8, 18, 28 or 38?

5. What year was the Calciopoli scandal uncovered?

6. Who is Napoli's record appearance holder?

7. Which team south of Rome has competed in the most Serie A seasons?

8. Who are the only Italian team to play in pink home shirts?

9. What club did Andrea Pirlo make his Serie A debut with?

10. How many times has Roma won Serie A? 1, 3, 5 or 7?

11. How many teams have played in Serie A? 56, 66, 76 or 86?

12. Which club, famous for their purple shirts, were the first-ever winners of the European Cup Winners' Cup in 1961?

13. After Juventus were relegated to Serie B, two players left to join rivals Inter. Name one.

14. In what year did Jose Mourinho win the treble with Inter?

15. Which club has Domenico Beradi spent almost his entire career at?

16. Which newly-promoted side did Franck Ribery join in 2021?

17. Who is the official sponsor of Serie A?

18. Who won the 2021 Serie A player of the year?

19. Who are Torino's city rivals?

20. What was the name of Napoli's stadium before it was renamed after club legend Diego Maradona?

1. Which German stadium was the first stadium in the world with a full colour changing exterior?

2. What is the primary colour of St Pauli's home shirts?

3. Roughly how much money did Michael Ballack pay as a fine to German authorities for failing to declare a handbag he had bought for his wife? £5k, £25k, £50k or £100k?

4. In 2015, how many minutes did it take Robert Lewandowski to score five goals for Bayern Münich against VfL Wolfsburg?

5. Which Bundesliga club did Kevin Keegan play for from 1977-80?

6. Surname of the identical twin brothers who made 543 Bundesliga appearances between them in the 2000s and 2010s and played for Turkey.

7. What Englishman joined Augsburg in 2019 from West Ham?

8. What nationally is goalkeeper Yann Sommer?

9. What number is on the Borussia Dortmund badge?

10. What does the RB in RB Leipzig stand for?

11. What division do Bundesliga clubs get relegated into?

12. What Champions League winner did Tony Pulis once say was "not at the required level" to play for West Brom in 2015?

13. Which team plays at the Olympiastadion?

14. Which Bavarian club won the first Bundesliga title?
(clue: it's not Bayern Munich!)

15. Which club is based in the city of Gelsenkirchen?

16. Costing £68m, who is the most expensive signing in Bundesliga history?

17. Which club is based by the Black Forest in the very south west of the country?

18. What two teams compete in the Nordderby (North Derby)?

19. Who scored the winner in the all Bundesliga Champions League final at Wembley in 2013?

20. Which Bundesliga team, nicknamed Kleeblätter (cloverleaves), have the smallest stadium in the 2021/22 season?

Round 18 - Ligue 1 II

1. How many seasons did Zlatan Ibrahimovic play in Ligue 1?

2. Which defender spent his entire professional career at Saint-Étienne making 470 appearances between 2003-2020?

3. Who was PSG's top scorer before the QSI takeover?

4. Name one of the two teams from the island of Corsica that have played in Ligue 1.

5. What season did Monaco last win Ligue 1?

6. Which team are Lille's fierce local rivals?

7. Which team is nicknamed 'Les Aiglons' (The Eagles) and boast Spaniard Joaquín Valle as their all-time leading goal scorer?

8. What decade was Ligue 1 formed? 1910s, 1920s, 1930s or 1940s?

9. Which Danish striker did Nice sign from Ajax in 2019?

10. What team has been in Ligue 1 for the longest time (over 70 seasons)?

11. How many winners of Ligue 1 has there been?
13, 23, 33 or 43?

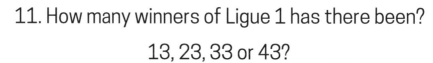

12. How many times has Marseille won Ligue 1? 3, 9, 18 or 27?

13. Which goalkeeper has made over 600 appearances for Marseille either side of a season at Crystal Palace in the 2016/17 season?

14. What is France's renowned national football centre called that has produced the likes of Kylian Mbappe, Thierry Henry and Nicolas Anelka among many others?

15. Which side won the Champions League but were relegated a year later?

16. Which team won the 1979 title, are based on the border with Germany and won promotion back to Ligue 1 in 2017?

17. Which Colchester-born goalkeeper broke into the Saint-Étienne first team in 2021?

18. Whom did Kylian Mbappe overtake as youngest Monaco goalscorer?

19. To the nearest 5,000, what is the capacity of the Stade Louis II stadium?

20. When did PSG win their first Ligue 1 title?
1980, 1982, 1984 or 1986?

1. What is the name of the Champions League anthem song?

2. Who is the only player to score in three separate Champions League finals?

3. Which three managers have won the Champions League three times?

4. Where was the 2019 Champions League final held?

5. Which was the first British stadium to host a Champions League final?

6. Who is the first player to play with seven different clubs in the Champions League group stage?

7. What brand is the Champions League ball?

8. Which Scandinavian team qualified for the 2021/22 group stage?

9. How many Champions Leagues has Pep Guardiola won as player and manager?

10. Who wrote the Champions League's famous anthem?

11. Who was the first player to get back-to-back hat-tricks doing so for Shakhtar Donetsk in 2014?

12. How many winners of the competition has Spain produced?

13. Which English team has won the Champions League, winning the fewest games?

14. Who scored the quickest Champions League goal after 10.2 seconds against Real Madrid in 2007?

15. Which team has reached the most consecutive Champions League Semi-finals, doing so from 2008-13?

16. All UEFA draws are currently held at UEFA headquarters in which Swiss municipality?

17. How many men have won the Champions League as players and managers?

18. Who was the first player to win the Champions League with two different teams consecutively doing so in 1993 and 1994?

19. Who scored the quickest goal in a Champions League final after 51 seconds?

20. Who scored a hat-trick for Real Madrid against PSG in the round of 16 second leg in 2022?

Next up is the Wiki game. Here you will have a snapshot of the Wikipedia pages from 20 players across different eras and you'll have to work out who they are based on their clubs, seasons and league stats across their whole club careers. Good luck!

Years	Team	Apps	(Gls)
2000–2001	Sporting CP B	16	(0)
2001–2003	Sporting CP	59	(8)
2003–2004	Barcelona	22	(1)
2004–2008	Porto	114	(24)
2008–2010	Inter Milan	24	(1)
2009	→ Chelsea (loan)	4	(0)
2010–2012	Beşiktaş	46	(8)
2013	Al-Ahli	10	(2)
2014–2015	Porto	42	(10)
2015–2019	Beşiktaş	108	(13)
2019–2020	Kasımpaşa	26	(4)
2020–	Vitória Guimarães	44	(5)

1)...

Years	Team	Apps	(Gls)
1984–1988	Newcastle United	92	(21)
1988–1992	Tottenham Hotspur	92	(19)
1992–1995	Lazio	43	(6)
1995–1998	Rangers	74	(30)
1998–2000	Middlesbrough	41	(4)
2000–2002	Everton	32	(1)
2002	Burnley	6	(0)
2003	Gansu Tianma	4	(2)
2004	Boston United	4	(0)
Total		**388**	**(83)**

2)...

Years	Team	Apps	(Gls)
1997–1999	Barcelona B	55	(3)
1998–2015	Barcelona	505	(58)
2015–2019	Al Sadd	82	(21)
Total		**642**	**(82)**

3)...

Years	Team	Apps	(Gls)
1932–1947	Stoke City	259	(51)
1947–1961	Blackpool	379	(17)
1961	→ Toronto City (loan)	14	(0)
1961–1965	Stoke City	59	(3)
1965	→ Toronto City (loan)	6	(0)
Total		**717**	**(71)**

4)...

Years	Team	Apps	(Gls)
1988–1989	Newell's Old Boys	24	(7)
1989–1990	River Plate	21	(4)
1990–1991	Boca Juniors	34	(13)
1991–2000	Fiorentina	269	(167)
2000–2003	Roma	63	(30)
2003	→ Inter Milan (loan)	12	(2)
2003–2005	Al-Arabi	21	(25)
Total		**444**	**(248)**

5)...

Years	Team	Apps	(Gls)
1979–1983	Partick Thistle	85	(41)
1983–1984	Watford	38	(23)
1984–1987	Celtic	99	(52)
1987–1989	Nantes	66	(22)
1989–1991	Rangers	76	(31)
1991–1993	Everton	34	(10)
1993–1995	Heart of Midlothian	35	(5)
1995–1996	Falkirk	41	(6)
1996–2001	Kansas City Wizards	149	(31)
Total		**623**	**(221)**

6)...

Years	Team	Apps	(Gls)
1995–1998	Brescia	47	(6)
1998–2001	Inter Milan	22	(0)
1999–2000	→ Reggina (loan)	28	(6)
2001	→ Brescia (loan)	10	(0)
2001–2011	AC Milan	284	(32)
2011–2015	Juventus	119	(16)
2015–2017	New York City FC	60	(1)
Total		**570**	**(61)**

7)...

Years	Team	Apps	(Gls)
1992–1993	Talleres	33	(1)
1993–1995	Banfield	66	(4)
1995–2014	Inter Milan	615	(12)
Total		**714**	**(17)**

8)...

Years	Team	Apps	(Gls)
1997–2002	Independiente	80	(37)
2002–2004	Manchester United	63	(10)
2004–2007	Villarreal	106	(54)
2007–2011	Atlético Madrid	134	(74)
2011–2012	Inter Milan	18	(2)
2012–2014	Internacional	34	(10)
2014–2015	Cerezo Osaka	42	(17)
2015–2016	Peñarol	30	(8)
2016	Mumbai City	11	(5)
2018	Kitchee	8	(5)
Total		**525**	**(222)**

9)...

Years	Team	Apps	(Gls)
1943–1956	Kispest Honvéd[i]	350	(358)
1958–1966	Real Madrid	180	(156)
Total		**530**	**(514)**

10)...

Years	Team	Apps	(Gls)
1964–1973	Ajax	240	(190)
1973–1978	Barcelona	143	(48)
1978–1979	Los Angeles Aztecs	23	(14)
1980–1981	Washington Diplomats	30	(12)
1981	Levante	10	(2)
1981–1983	Ajax	36	(14)
1983–1984	Feyenoord	33	(11)
Total		**514**	**(291)**

11)...

Years	Team	Apps	(Gls)
1949–1957	Leeds United	297	(157)
1957–1962	Juventus	155	(108)
1962	Leeds United	11	(3)
1962–1963	Roma	10	(4)
1963–1966	Cardiff City	69	(18)
1966–1971	Hereford United	173	(80)
1972–1974	Merthyr Tydfil		
Total		**715**	**(370)**

12)...

Years	Team	Apps	(Gls)
2002–2003	RS Futebol	25	(2)
2003–2004	Juventude	35	(3)
2004–2006	Porto B	14	(0)
2005–2006	→ Dynamo Moscow (loan)	0	(0)
2006–2009	Fluminense	108	(9)
2009–2012	AC Milan	93	(5)
2012–2020	Paris Saint-Germain	204	(9)
2020–	Chelsea	43	(5)

13)...

Years	Team	Apps	(Gls)
1977–1990	Spartak Moscow	344	(86)
1990–1991	Red Star Saint-Ouen	15	(1)
1991–1993	Spartak Moscow	54	(9)
Total		**413**	**(96)**

14)...

Years	Team	Apps	(Gls)
2006–2007	Bayern Munich II	42	(5)
2007–2009	Bayern Munich	1	(0)
2008–2009	→ Borussia Dortmund (loan)	13	(0)
2009–2016	Borussia Dortmund	212	(19)
2016–2019	Bayern Munich	74	(3)
2019–	Borussia Dortmund	81	(7)

15)...

Years	Team	Apps	(Gls)
1976–1981	Argentinos Juniors	166	(116)
1981–1982	Boca Juniors	40	(28)
1982–1984	Barcelona	36	(22)
1984–1991	Napoli	188	(81)
1992–1993	Sevilla	26	(5)
1993–1994	Newell's Old Boys	5	(0)
1995–1997	Boca Juniors	30	(7)
Total		**491**	**(259)**

16)...

Years	Team	Apps	(Gls)
1999–2000	Bayer Leverkusen II	28	(9)
2000–2005	Bayer Leverkusen	7	(0)
2001–2004	→ San Jose Earthquakes (loan)	87	(32)
2005–2014	LA Galaxy	247	(112)
2009	→ Bayern Munich (loan)	6	(0)
2010	→ Everton (loan)	10	(2)
2012	→ Everton (loan)	7	(0)
2016	LA Galaxy	6	(1)
2018	León	6	(0)
2019	San Diego Sockers (indoor)	8	(5)
Total		**412**	**(161)**

17)...

Years	Team	Apps	(Gls)
2003–2004	1. FC Köln II	2	(0)
2003–2006	1. FC Köln	81	(46)
2006–2009	Bayern Munich	71	(15)
2007–2008	Bayern Munich II	2	(0)
2009–2012	1. FC Köln	88	(33)
2012–2015	Arsenal	60	(19)
2015	→ Inter Milan (loan)	17	(1)
2015–2017	Galatasaray	56	(20)
2017–2020	Vissel Kobe	52	(15)
2020–2021	Antalyaspor	40	(6)
2021–	Górnik Zabrze	15	(4)

18)...

Years	Team	Apps	(Gls)
1997–2000	Metz	47	(5)
1999	→ Newcastle United (loan)	11	(1)
2000–2004	Fulham	117	(53)
2004–2008	Manchester United	86	(28)
2008–2012	Everton	97	(27)
2012	Tottenham Hotspur	10	(3)
2012–2013	Sunderland	11	(0)
2013	Lazio	6	(0)
Total		**385**	**(117)**

19)...

Years	Team	Apps	(Gls)
2002–2004	Universidad Católica	42	(13)
2004–2006	Albacete	25	(5)
2006–2007	Liverpool	25	(2)
2006	→ Real Sociedad (loan)	16	(6)
2007–2009	Betis	44	(10)
2009–2014	CSKA Moscow	49	(6)
2014–2015	Universidad Católica	41	(14)
2016	Sport Recife	8	(1)
2017	Colo-Colo	4	(0)
2018–2019	Magallanes	20	(5)
Total		**274**	**(62)**

20)...

Can you match these clubs and national
teams with their respective stadiums?

Athletic Bilbao	Mercedes-Benz Stadium
Atlanta United	Stadio Artemio Franchi
Atletico Madrid	Fisht Olympic Stadium
Basel	Wanda Metropolitano
Colorado Rapids	Mercedes-Benz Arena
Exeter City	St. Jakob-Park
Fiorentina	Krestovsky Stadium
Iran	Deepdale
Kaiserslautern	St James' Park
Marseille	Fritz-Walter-Stadion
Newcastle United	San Mames
Porto	St James Park
Preston North End	Stade Velodrome
River Plate	Dicks Sporting Goods Park
Sochi	El Madrigal
Stuttgart	El Monumental
Udinese	Azadi Stadium
Villareal	Racecourse Ground
Wrexham	Stadio Friuli
Zenit St Petersburg	Estádio do Dragão

1. Which country has won the most World Cups with five?

2. Where was the first World Cup held?

3. Who hosted the 1958 World Cup?

4. Which referee gave Croatia's Josip Šimunić three yellow cards before sending him off in 2006?

5. Who scored the winner for Germany in the 2014 World Cup Final?

6. Who is the World Cup all-time top goal scorer?

7. In which World Cup did Diego Maradona score his famous 'Hand of God' goal?

8. Name both teams who made their World Cup debuts in 2018.

9. Who is the only player to win three World Cups?

10. How many times have England hosted the World Cup?

11. Which CONCACAF nation has lost the most matches in the World Cup finals?

12. In 2002, which goalkeeper saved a record 2 penalties in one World Cup (excluding penalty shoot-outs)?

13. Which famous stadium was the first to host two World Cup Finals?

14. Which team has lost the most penalty shootouts in World Cup history with three?

15. Which team beat West Germany 1-0 in the highly anticipated last game of Group 1 in the 1974 finals?

16. What was the name of the dog who found the 1966 World Cup trophy?

17. Which four times winners has drawn the most World Cup games?

18. The highest scoring game in World Cup history was between Switzerland and Austria in 1954 containing 12 goals. What was the score?

19. Which South American nation has the most World Cup yellow and red cards?

20. Which Cameroonian is the oldest World Cup goalscorer?

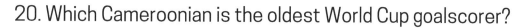

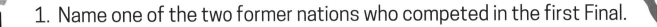

1. Name one of the two former nations who competed in the first Final.

2. How many teams are in the Euros?

3. When was the first Euros?

4. What city hosted the Euro 2020 Euro Final?

5. Which two teams have won the Euros the most times with three?

6. Who scored the winning goal in the 2016 final?

7. Who has scored the most Euro goals?

8. How often is the Euros held?

9. Who is the trophy named after?

10. How many times has France won the Euros?

11. Which Spanish goalkeeper has the most clean sheets in Euro history with 9?

12. Who is the only manager to win the Euros with a country other than his own?

13. Which player scored the iconic winning penalty in the 1976 Final for Czechoslovakia against Germany?

14. Which German has managed the most games at the Euros?

15. Who scored the most goals in a single Euro competition with nine?

16. Who is the only player to score in two Euro finals?

17. What manager took Wales to the 2016 Euros Semi-final?

18. What two countries hosted the 2000 Euros?

19. What country caused one of the biggest shocks in football history by winning Euro 2004?

20. Name the two countries that made its Euros debut in 2020?

1. When was the first Copa América held?

1916, 1926, 1936 or 1946?

2. Which two teams has won the most Copa Américas?

3. Brazil beat which host nation, whom they share a border with, in the 1997 Final? Bolivia, Colombia, Paraguay or Venezuela?

4. How many Copa Américas has Lionel Messi won?

5. Venezuela was the last CONMEBOL nation to host the tournament, what year did they first host? 1977, 1987, 1997 or 2007?

6. Which nation hosted the first Copa América outside of South America in 2016?

7. Uruguay have never lost one of the seven tournaments they've hosted. True or false?

8. What country hosted the 2021 Copa América?

9. How many countries played in the 2021 edition?

10. What animal was the 2021 Copa América mascot?

Cat, Dog, Leopard or Jaguar?

11. Which middle east nation was invited to the 2019 edition?

12. Three South American teams have lost more finals than they've won. Chile, Paraguay and who?

13. Which team won back-to-back Copa Américas on penalties in 2015 and 2016 both against Argentina?

14. Which side won their first and only title in 2001 after defender Iván Córdoba scored the winner in the final against Mexico?

15. How many Copa Américas did Diego Maradona win?

16. What is the biggest victory in a final, coming in 1949 when Brazil beat Paraguay? 7-0, 8-0, 8-1 or 9-1?

17. Which Asian nation was invited in 1999 and 2019?

18. Which Everton player scored the third Brazil goal in the 2019 Final?

19. Who is Peru's all-time leading goalscorer who was included in the 2011, 2015 and 2019 team of the tournaments?

20. Which was the first non-South American nation to reach the final? USA, Japan, Spain or Mexico?

1. What does AFCON stand for?

2. Who won the 2021 AFCON?

3. When was the first AFCON tournament?
1957, 1967, 1977 or 1987?

4. Which Cameroonian has scored the most AFCON goals?

5. How many AFCON tournaments has Didier Drogba won?

6. What country does Nicolas Pepe represent?

7. Which county has won the most AFCON titles with seven?

8. How many countries have played in AFCON? 24, 34, 44 or 54?

9. How many countries play in AFCON tournaments?

10. How many AFCON titles have Nigeria won? 1, 3, 5 or 7?

11. Who are the only nation to win three titles in a row, doing
so in 2006, 2008 and 2010?

12. Name one of the two CECAFA (East Africa) sides who have won the tournament.

13. Which French manager won the 2012 and 2015 editions with two different teams?

14. Which Senegal player won the 2021 most valuable player?

15. Which Egyptian striker scored 11 goals in six tournaments ranging from 1986 and 2006?

16. Who captained Zambia to victory in the 2012 AFCON?

17. Which Zambian striker joined Southampton after helping his country win the 2012 tournament?

18. Which side has made the most consecutive appearances with 15 between 1994 and 2019, winning the 2004 edition?

19. What national side did former Manchester United striker Manucho represent?

20. Which French manager has managed six different teams at AFCON?

1. How often is the Gold Cup held?

2. What country has won the most Gold Cups with 8?

3. How many countries compete in the Gold Cup?

4. When was the Gold Cup founded? 1951, 1971, 1991 or 2001?

5. Which American is the Gold Cup's top goalscorer with 18 goals?

6. What is the biggest margin of victory in a final when Mexico beat the US in 2009? 3-0, 4-0, 5-0 or 6-0?

7. How many Gold Cups have the US won?

8. Since 2000, the Gold Cup has aired live on which stations sports channel? CNBC, CNN, FOX or MSNBC?

9. In 2013, a play-off was played to determine CONCACAFs entry into what international tournament?

10. Who won the first Gold Cup?

11. What is the only Caribbean country to host Gold Cup games?

12. Which African side was invited to play the 2005 edition?

13. Brazil has been invited three times, how many titles have they won?

14. Who are the only nation to win the Gold Cup other than the US and Mexico?

15. Which Mexican scored a stunning chip against Tim Howard in the 2011 Final?

16. Which Asian side finished 4th at the 2002 edition?

17. What does CONCACAF stand for?

18. Which Central American side won the predecessor CONCACAF Championships three times?

19. The top scorer in the inaugural CONCACAF Championship in 1961 was called Eduardo "_____" Hernández? Audi, BMW, Mercedes, or Volkswagen?

20. When did the US play their first CONCACAF Championship? 1970, 1975, 1980 or 1985?

1. Which country has won the most Asia Cups with four?

2. How many countries are eligible to register for the Asia Cup? 38, 42, 46 or 50?

3. How many countries play in the Asia Cup finals?

4. When was the first Asia Cup held? 1954, 1964, 1974 or 1984?

5. Which microstate hosted the first Asia Cup?

6. The Khmer Republic finished fourth in the fifth edition of the tournament, what is the name of the nation today?

7. Which side reached five finals in a row between 1984 and 2000 winning three?

8. Which former winner of the Asian Cup is now a member of UEFA?

9. Which Middle East side won their first Asian Cup in 2019?

10. How many times have China won the competition?

11. Which Australian, who went on to manage Celtic, won the 2015 edition as manager?

12. Which former CSKA Moscow and AC Milan free-kick specialist won the 2011 best player award for Japan?

13. Which team left the OFC to join the AFC in 2006?

14. Who, in 2012, became the first team to win the OFC Nations Cup other than Australia and New Zealand?

15. Which host nation lost to New Zealand on penalties in the 2016 edition? Fiji, Papua New Guinea, Solomon Islands or Vanuatu?

16. When was the first OFC Nations Cup held? 1973, 1983, 1993 or 2003?

17. Which Pacific island nation has reached the most OFC finals without winning?

18. Which striker, who signed for Newcastle in 2022, scored a hat-trick for New Zealand in the 2012 edition?

19. Which striker signed for Everton after winning the 2004 OFC Nations Cup with Australia?

20. Which former Oldham, Celtic and Middlesbrough striker has scored 7 goals for New Zealand in the OFC Nations Cup?

1. Name one of the two 1978 Argentinian World Cup winners who made surprise moves to Spurs.

2. Who has scored the most goals in a World Cup final?

3. Name one of the two players who won the 1994 and 2002 World Cup.

4. What Brazilian player has the most assists in World Cup history with 10?

5. Considered the greatest South American defender of all time, who is the only man to win two World Cups with Argentina?

6. Which English goalkeeper has the most clean sheets with 10?

7. Which Argentinian has received the most cards in World Cup history?

8. Only four European players have won more than one World Cup and they all played for which country?

9. What country has played at every World Cup Finals?

10. To the nearest 500 million, how many people watched the 2018 World Cup?

11. Who captained Brazil to victory in the 1970 World Cup, scoring the fourth goal in the final, considered one of the greatest goals in the history of the tournament?

12. Doing so in 1994, which Russian striker has scored the most goals in one World Cup game with 5?

13. How many World Cups did Gianluigi Buffon participate in?

14. Which country has lost the most World Cup finals?

15. Which member of Italy's 2006 World Cup Final starting XI was born in Argentina?

16. Which Argentinian is the only player to score a hat-trick at two separate World Cups?

17. Which German player has the most World Cup appearances with 25?

18. Who was the Dutch goalkeeper for the 2010 World Cup Final?

19. Which German centre-back who won the World Cup in 2014 was born on a leap year day (29th February)?

20. Which former Blackburn and Stoke midfielder won the 2018 World Cup with France?

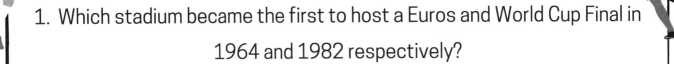

1. Which stadium became the first to host a Euros and World Cup Final in 1964 and 1982 respectively?

2. What was the name of the stadium shared by Torino and Juventus from 1990-2006 which is Italian for 'Stadium of the Alps'?

3. What team plays at the Signal Iduna Park?

4. Who were the tenants at Anfield before Liverpool?

5. What team plays at Estadio da Luz?

6. What is the name of Boca Juniors stadium, meaning chocolate box in Spanish?

7. Where do Norwich play their home games?

8. What was Arsenal's home from 1913-2006 called?

9. When did the new Wembley stadium open?

10. What city is Villa Park located in?

11. The 114,000 capacity Rungrado 1st of May stadium is in what country?

12. What is the capacity of the Nou Camp to the nearest thousand?

13. What US state is the famous Rose Bowl stadium located in?

14. Name one of the two club teams who play at the iconic Maracanã Stadium.

15. What is the second biggest stadium in the Premier League?

16. What team plays at the Johan Cruyff Arena?

17. Who was Atlético Madrid's stadium until 2016 named after?

18. What South African city is Soccer city based in?

19. What was the capacity of the old Wembley Stadium?

20. Which stadium hosted the 2018 World Cup Final?

1. Who crossed the ball to assist Messi's header against Manchester United in the 2009 Champions League Final?

2. He scored a Maradona-esque goal against which club in 2007?

3. How many Balon d'Ors has he won?

4. What brand of boots does he wear?

5. How many La Liga titles has he won?

6. What youth club did Barcelona sign him from?

7. Who were the other two members of Barcelona's attacking trio 'MSN'?

8. What is his middle name?

9. How tall is he?

10. How many Champions Leagues has he won?

11. What was his first contract famously signed on?

12. At what age did he win his first Ballon d'Or?

13. At what Olympics did he win gold for Argentina?

14. What is his original nickname?

15. Which English club made an offer for him whilst he was in Barcelona's youth team?

16. What city was he born in?

17. How many red cards has he received? 1, 2, 3 or 4?

18. His descendants came from Catalonia and which European country?

19. What year was he born?

20. What religion is he?

1. What year did he first sign for Manchester United?

2. What team has he played the most games for?

3. What brand of boots does Cristiano Ronaldo wear?

4. Which club did Manchester United sign Cristiano Ronaldo from in 2003?

5. In 2021, what Manchester United player allowed him to have the number seven shirt?

6. How many Champions Leagues has he won?

7. How many times has he won the Balon d'Or?

8. What shirt number did he wear in his first season at Real Madrid?

9. What is the name of his eldest son?

10. How tall is he?

11. What city and/or island was he born in?

12. Who injured him in the 2016 Euro final?

13. What year was he born?

14. To the nearest million, how much did Manchester United pay for him as an 18-year-old?

15. His £80m transfer to Real Madrid broke the world record set by which player in the same transfer window?

16. Who did he surpass to become Real Madrid's top scorer?

17. What brand of drink did he famously remove from the table before a press conference?

18. He became the Champions League's all-time leading goal scorer after a hat-trick against which eastern European side?

19. What round of the Champions League did he score the famous bicycle kick against Juventus in 2018?

20. Before his transfer to Juventus, which player signed by Barcelona in 2017, was the most expensive over 30 player of all-time?

1. Who is the all-time leading goal scorer with 53 goals?

2. Where do England play their home games?

3. Who captained England at Euro 2020?

4. Who has the most caps for England with 125?

5. Who did England play in the 2018 World Cup semi-final, their first in 28 years?

6. Who was the youngest player to play for England at 17 years 74 days?

7. Other than Geoff Hurst, who is the only England player to score in a World Cup Final?

8. Which Wolverhampton Wanderers one-club man was the first footballer to earn 100 international caps?

9. Who was England's first full-time manager?

10. Who was manager for the team that hosted Euro '96?

11. Who has England played the most games against with 115 including their first?

12. How many England players have over 100 caps for England? 7, 9, 11 or 13?

13. Who is the youngest ever goalscorer?

14. Who is the highest-scoring England defender?

15. Which English company supplied England kits from 1974-84?

16. What colour were England's first away kits?

17. What is the lowest England have ever ranked in the FIFA rankings? 21st, 23rd, 25th or 27th?

18. What was the score for England's biggest ever win which came against Ireland in 1882? 9-0, 11-0, 13-0 or 15-0?

19. Which team, nicknamed the 'Magic Magyars', inflicted England's biggest ever defeat of 7-1 in 1954?

20. England had two players sent off in a match for the first time against which opposition in 2020?

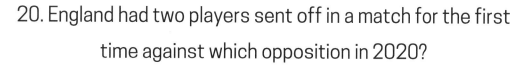

Here is part II of the Wiki game!

Years	Team	Apps	(Gls)
1968–1971	Scunthorpe United	124	(18)
1971–1977	Liverpool	230	(68)
1977–1980	Hamburger SV	90	(32)
1980–1982	Southampton	68	(37)
1982–1984	Newcastle United	78	(48)
1985	Blacktown City	2	(1)
Total		**592**	**(204)**

1)...

Years	Team	Apps	(Gls)
1953–1957	Millwall	105	(2)
1957–1969	Sunderland	402	(23)
1969–1971	Bolton Wanderers	43	(3)
Total		**550**	**(28)**

2)...

Years	Team	Apps	(Gls)
1999–2001	Lanceros Boyacá	13	(5)
2004–2009	River Plate	90	(34)
2009–2011	Porto	51	(41)
2011–2013	Atlético Madrid	68	(52)
2013–2019	Monaco	108	(65)
2014–2015	→ Manchester United (loan)	25	(4)
2015–2016	→ Chelsea (loan)	10	(1)
2019–2021	Galatasaray	34	(19)
2021–	Rayo Vallecano	14	(5)

3)...

Years	Team	Apps	(Gls)
1996–2000	Sydney Olympic	94	(16)
2000–2003	Feyenoord	92	(11)
2003–2011	Blackburn Rovers	247	(13)
2011–2014	Sydney FC	57	(7)
Total		**490**	**(47)**

4)...

Years	Team	Apps	(Gls)
1964–1977	Bayern Munich	427	(60)
1977–1980	New York Cosmos	80	(17)
1980–1982	Hamburger SV	28	(0)
1983	New York Cosmos	25	(2)
Total		**560**	**(79)**

5)...

Years	Team	Apps	(Gls)
1957–1960	Sporting Lourenço Marques	42	(77)
1961–1975	Benfica	301	(317)
1975	Boston Minutemen	7	(2)
1975	Monterrey	10	(1)
1975–1976	Toronto Metros-Croatia	21	(16)
1976	Beira-Mar	12	(3)
1976–1977	Las Vegas Quicksilvers	17	(2)
1977–1978	União de Tomar	12	(3)
1978–1979	New Jersey Americans	9	(2)
1979–1980	Buffalo Stalions (indoor)	5	(1)
Total		**436**	**(424)**

6)...

Years	Team	Apps	(Gls)
2004	Chico Rooks	16	(17)
2005	San Jose Earthquakes	2	(0)
2006–2009	Houston Dynamo	37	(4)
2009–2021	San Jose Earthquakes	374	(167)
Total		**429**	**(188)**

7)...

Years	Team	Apps	(Gls)
2004–2007	Nagoya Grampus Eight	90	(11)
2008–2009	VVV-Venlo	68	(24)
2010–2013	CSKA Moscow	94	(20)
2014–2017	AC Milan	81	(11)
2017–2018	Pachuca	29	(10)
2018–2019	Melbourne Victory	18	(7)
2019	Vitesse	4	(0)
2020	Botafogo	22	(3)
2021	Neftçi Baku	7	(2)
2021–	FK Sūduva	6	(1)

8)...

Years	Team	Apps	(Gls)
1993–1995	Sport Recife	24	(3)
1995–2001	Vasco da Gama	188	(38)
2001–2009	Lyon	248	(75)
2009–2011	Al-Gharafa	40	(15)
2011–2012	Vasco da Gama	63	(15)
2013	New York Red Bulls	13	(0)
2013	Vasco da Gama	21	(2)
Total		**597**	**(148)**

9)...

Years	Team	Apps	(Gls)
1950–1970	Dynamo Moscow	326	(0)

10)...

Years	Team	Apps	(Gls)
1991–1996	Nancy	243	(98)
1996–1997	Sporting CP	27	(3)
1997–1999	Deportivo	31	(2)
1999–2001	Coventry City	62	(12)
2001–2004	Aston Villa	35	(2)
2004	Espanyol	16	(1)
2004–2005	Emirates Club	15	(5)
2005–2007	1. FC Saarbrücken	54	(10)
2007–2010	Fola Esch	44	(25)
Total		**518**	**(155)**

11)...

Years	Team	Apps	(Gls)
1989–1995	Sporting CP	129	(16)
1995–2000	Barcelona	172	(30)
2000–2005	Real Madrid	164	(38)
2005–2009	Inter Milan	105	(9)
Total		**570**	**(93)**

12)...

Years	Team	Apps	(Gls)
1982–1984	Hebar	32	(14)
1984–1990	CSKA Sofia	119	(81)
1990–1995	Barcelona	151	(76)
1995–1996	Parma	23	(5)
1996–1998	Barcelona	24	(7)
1998	Al-Nassr	2	(1)
1998–1999	Kashiwa Reysol	27	(12)
2000–2002	Chicago Fire	51	(17)
2003	D.C. United	21	(5)
Total		**454**	**(220)**

13)...

Years	Team	Apps	(Gls)
1997	Toronto Lynx	7	(3)
1997–1999	FSV Zwickau	12	(1)
1999–2000	Richmond Kickers	35	(17)
2001–2005	San Jose Earthquakes	108	(27)
2006–2008	Houston Dynamo	78	(24)
2009–2011	Toronto FC	57	(27)
2011	New York Red Bulls	13	(2)
2011–2013	D.C. United	68	(23)
2014	Toronto FC	19	(1)
2018–2019	Mississauga MetroStars (indoor)	11	(8)
Total		**408**	**(133)**

14)...

Years	Team	Apps	(Gls)
1995–1998	Bellmare Hiratsuka	85	(16)
1998–2000	Perugia	48	(12)
2000–2001	Roma	30	(5)
2001–2004	Parma	67	(5)
2004	→ Bologna (loan)	17	(2)
2004–2006	Fiorentina	20	(0)
2005–2006	→ Bolton Wanderers (loan)	21	(1)
Total		**288**	**(41)**

15)...

Years	Team	Apps	(Gls)
1939–1959	Wolverhampton Wanderers	490	(13)

16)...

Years	Team	Apps	(Gls)
1969–1988	Dynamo Kyiv	432	(211)
1988–1989	Vorwärts Steyr	41	(9)
1989–1990	Aris Limassol	22	(5)
Total		**495**	**(225)**

17)...

Years	Team	Apps	(Gls)
1997–1999	Sporting CP	53	(12)
1999–2001	Barcelona	46	(3)
2001–2007	Benfica	172	(75)
2007–2010	Atlético Madrid	113	(20)
2011–2012	Beşiktaş	46	(8)
2012–2014	Espanyol	60	(3)
2015	NorthEast United	10	(3)
Total		**500**	**(124)**

18)...

Years	Team	Apps	(Gls)
1958–1974	West Ham United	544	(24)
1974–1977	Fulham	124	(1)
1976	→ San Antonio Thunder (loan)	24	(1)
1978	Seattle Sounders	7	(0)
1978	Herning Fremad	9	(0)
1983	Carolina Lightnin'	8	(0)
Total		**719**	**(26)**

19)...

Years	Team	Apps	(Gls)
1979–1984	Borussia Mönchengladbach	162	(36)
1984–1988	Bayern Munich	113	(57)
1988–1992	Inter Milan	115	(40)
1992–2000	Bayern Munich	189	(28)
2000	MetroStars	16	(0)
2018	1. FC Herzogenaurach	1	(0)
Total		**596**	**(161)**

20)...

1. Uruguay v Brazil
1950
World Cup Final

2. Barcelona v Bayern Munich
2020
Champions League Quarter-final

3. Liverpool v Arsenal
1989
First Division

4. Portugal v North Korea
1966
World Cup Quarter-final

5. Australia v American Samoa
2001
World Cup Qualifiers

6. England v West Germany
1966
World Cup Final

7. Middlesbrough v Manchester City
2008
Premier League

8. Tottenham Hotspur v Arsenal
2004
Premier League

9. Monaco v Deportivo La Coruna
2003
Champions League Groups

10. Italy v Brazil
1982
World Cup Second Stage

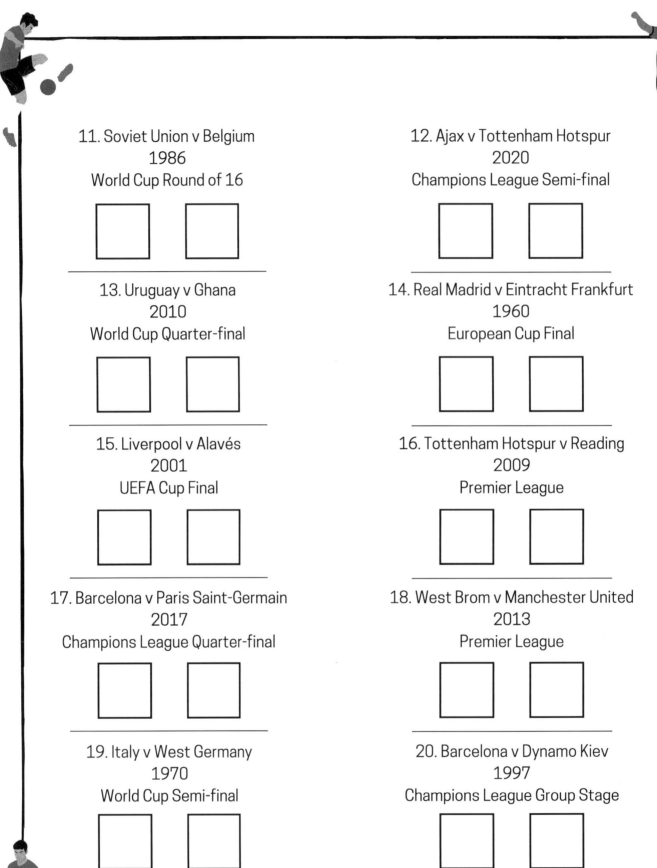

11. Soviet Union v Belgium
1986
World Cup Round of 16

12. Ajax v Tottenham Hotspur
2020
Champions League Semi-final

13. Uruguay v Ghana
2010
World Cup Quarter-final

14. Real Madrid v Eintracht Frankfurt
1960
European Cup Final

15. Liverpool v Alavés
2001
UEFA Cup Final

16. Tottenham Hotspur v Reading
2009
Premier League

17. Barcelona v Paris Saint-Germain
2017
Champions League Quarter-final

18. West Brom v Manchester United
2013
Premier League

19. Italy v West Germany
1970
World Cup Semi-final

20. Barcelona v Dynamo Kiev
1997
Champions League Group Stage

Round 35 - Women's Football

1. When was the Women's football association formed?
1909, 1929, 1949 or 1969?

2. Who won the 2021 Women's Balon d'Or?

3. What bank sponsors the Women's Super League?

4. When was the women's Champions League formed?
1995, 1997, 1999 or 2001?

5. What team has won the most Champions Leagues?

6. Who won the 2021 Champions League?

7. Who is England's all-time leading goal scorer with 48 goals?

8. What nationality is Ada Hegerberg, the first-ever recipient of the Ballon d'Or Féminin?

9. Who is the most successful Women's World Cup team with four titles?

10. Who was England manager from 1998-2013?

11. Which Dutchwoman has scored the most Super League goals of all time?

12. How many teams are in the Super League? 8, 12, 16 or 20?

13. When was the first season of the Women's Super League? 2011, 2013, 2015 or 2017?

14. Which Brazilian is a six-time FIFA World Player of the Year and is often regarded as the greatest female player of all-time?

15. Which England and Lyon right-back came second in the 2019 Ballon d'Or Féminin?

16. Which US striker imitated drinking a cup of tea after scoring against England in the 2019 World Cup semi-final?

17. Which Canadian has scored the most international goals of all-time with 188?

18. Who has been Chelsea manager since 2012?

19. Kristine Lilly is the most capped footballer of all time, how many caps did she win? 154, 254, 354 or 454?

20. Who is the US' all-time leading goalscorer?

1. If a player is sent off, which card is shown to the player?

2. How many official laws are there in football?
   17, 170, 1,700 or 17,000?

3. How far away is the edge of the penalty area from the goal line?

4. How long is added on to the game in extra time?

5. What is the minimum length of a soccer pitch?

6. What is the maximum length of a football pitch?

7. How many officials are there on a match day (excluding VAR)?

8. What is the minimum number of players for one team before they must forfeit?

9. What is the official match ball size of a professional soccer ball?

10. How far away is the penalty spot from the goal?

11. What is the official size of goalposts in soccer?

12. What does VAR stand for?

13. How far away must opposition players stand from a defending team's free-kick wall?

14. How tall must corner flags be (to the nearest foot)?

15. How heavy must a ball be before kickoff (to the nearest 100g)?

16. How long does halftime last?

17. Substitutions during matches in the English Football League were first officially permitted when? 1935, 1945, 1955 or 1965?

18. What is the name of the goal line technology used in the Premier League called?

19. What is a silver goal?

20. What is the term for a free kick you cannot score from?

Lastly, here are a few 50/50s to finish off, good luck!

1. Which club is the furthest east, Celtic or Rangers?

2. Which club is furthest north, Arsenal or Spurs?

3. Which Sheffield club has more First Division titles, United or Wednesday?

4. Whose record transfer is higher, Burnley or Norwich?

5. Who scored more Premier League goals, Frank Lampard or Thierry Henry?

6. Who has more England caps, Gordon Banks or Joe Hart?

7. Who has managed more Premier League games, Sir Alex Ferguson or Arsène Wenger?

8. Who cost Real Madrid more, Gareth Bale or Eden Hazard?

9. Who retired first, Paulo Maldini or Javier Zanetti?

10. Who made their Premier League debut at a later age, Ian Wright or Jamie Vardy?

11. Who made more appearances for Barcelona, Xavi or Iniesta?

12. Who has reached more World Cup Finals? Spain or Hungary?

13. Who has scored more World Cup goals,
Gabriel Batistuta or Diego Maradona?

14. Whose highest ever FIFA world ranking is higher, Scotland or Wales?

15. Which team have lost more Champions League finals,
Ajax or Bayern Munich?

16. Who has won more Champions League titles, Manchester City or Steaua
Bucureşti?

17. Who has won more MLS Cups, New York City or New York Red Bulls?

18. Who has won more Copa Libertadores titles, São Paulo or Corinthians?

19. Who scored more goals in the A-League,
Alessandro Del Piero or David Villa?

20. Who has won more Champions League titles,
Liverpool or Manchester United?

ANSWERS

Warm-Up
1. Argentinian
2. France
3. Black
4. Manchester United
5. Bayern Munich
6. Liverpool
7. Neymar
8. Manchester City
9. Johan Cruyff
10. Portugal

Round 1 - Premier League
1. Sheffield United
2. Aston Villa
3. Alan Shearer
4. Southampton
5. Everton, Liverpool, Arsenal, Tottenham, Liverpool, Manchester United
6. Thomas Frank
7. David Moyes
8. 14
9. Thierry Henry
10. Pepe Reina
11. 4th minute of stoppage time (93:20)
12. Branislav Ivanović
13. Gareth Barry
14. Burnley, 107 matches.
15. 1992
16. Everton
17. James Vaughan
18. Sadio Mane
19. 22
20. Portsmouth vs Reading, 7-4, 29th September 2007

Round 2 - La Liga
1. Lionel Messi
2. Athletic Bilbao
3. Real Betis
4. Racing Club
5. Deportivo La Coruña
6. Barcelona
7. Levante
8. Athletic Bilbao
9. Real Sociedad
10. 1920s
11. Spanish Civil War
12. 9
13. 48
14. Rafael Benitez
15. El Clasico
16. Andoni Zubizarreta
17. Karim Benzema
18. Joaquin Sanchez
19. Raúl
20. 6

Round 3 - Serie A
1. Juventus
2. Silvio Piola
3. Gianluigi Buffon
4. The Old Lady
5. 1898
6. Stadio Giuseppe Meazza
7. 7
8. Green and Black
9. Torino
10. Genoa
11. Coppa Italia
12. Cagliari
13. Brazil
14. Alessandro Del Piero
15. Sven-Göran Eriksson
16. Inter Milan
17. Shield
18. 2000/01
19. Fikayo Tomori
20. Dušan Vlahović

Round 4 - Bundesliga

1. Gerd Müller
2. 1963
3. Borussia Mönchengladbach
4. Werder Bremen
5. Three
6. Charly Körbel
7. 34
8. Wolfsburg
9. Stuttgart
10. Köln/Cologne
11. Claudio Pizarro
12. Union Berlin
13. Three
14. 2012
15. Schalke 04
16. Federal League
17. Bavaria
18. Erling Haaland
19. 0, free transfer
20. Ballspiel-Verein Borussia

Round 5 - Ligue 1

1. Lille
2. Saint-Étienne
3. Reims
4. Joey Barton
5. 1970
6. 2009/10
7. 2002
8. 32
9. Uber Eats
10. Montpellier
11. Edison Cavani
12. Monaco
13. Delio Onnis
14. 5-5
15. Jean-Pierre Papin
16. Mickaël Landreau
17. Lyon
18. L'Hexagoal
19. Nantes
20. 74

Round 6 - European Leagues

1. Benfica
2. Anzhi Makhachkala
3. Boavista
4. Djibril Cissé
5. Galatasaray
6. Olympiacos
7. Brøndby
8. Pro League
9. Liechtenstein
10. 18
11. Young Boys
12. Red Star v Partizan Belgrade
13. Ajax
14. Hadjuk Split
15. Shakhtar Donetsk
16. Spartak Moscow
17. Hristo Stoichkov
18. Kharkiv
19. Grasshopper
20. Hakan Şükür

Round 7 - MLS

1. Most-Valuable-Player
2. Zlatan Ibrahimović
3. 28
4. 2018
5. Landon Donovan
6. LA Galaxy
7. 3
8. David Beckham
9. Carlos Vela, 34
10. Supporters Shield
11. New York City FC
12. Inter Miami FC
13. New York Red Bulls
14. Josef Martinez
15. Dallas FC
16. Vancouver Whitecaps
17. Toronto FC
18. 1996
19. San Jose Earthquakes
20. Montreal

Round 8 - Champions League

1. Real Madrid
2. Cristiano Ronaldo
3. Alfredo Di Stefano
4. Lucas Moura
5. 1992
6. Clarence Seedorf
7. James Milner (2017/18)
8. 32
9. Istanbul
10. Five
11. Rubin Kazan
12. Juventus
13. Faroe Islands, Gibraltar, Iceland, Malta.
14. Zero
15. Atlético Madrid
16. Ferenc Puskás
17. Nottingham Forest
18. 22
19. Porto
20. Thierry Henry

Round 9 - Europa League

1. Sevilla
2. 32
3. 5th
4. Four
5. Villareal
6. Portugal
7. José Antonio Reyes
8. Benfica
9. Club Brugge
10. Galatasaray
11. Arsenal & Chelsea
12. Henrik Larsson
13. Baku
14. Ajax
15. Two
16. Radamel Falcao
17. Wolverhampton Wanderers
18. Italian
19. Inter Milan
20. Zenit St Petersburg

Round 10 - English Football League

1. 72
2. Northampton Town
3. Five
4. Four
5. Four
6. Sylvan Ebanks-Blake
7. Tiger
8. Jay Bothroyd
9. Coca Cola
10. Reading
11. Wigan Athletic
12. Swindon Town
13. Quest
14. Stadium of Light
15. 2004
16. 1888
17. Burnley, Wolves, Preston North End
18. Plymouth Argyle
19. 46
20. Billy Sharp

Round 11 - English Domestic Cups

1. Arsenal, 14
2. Carling Cup
3. Dave Beasant
4. 1960
5. 1870s (1872)
6. Ashley Cole, 7
7. 2016
8. Ian Rush, 5
9. £100,000
10. West Ham United
11. Manchester City
12. Didier Drogba
13. Cardiff City
14. Lincoln City v Burnley
15. Kepa Arrizabalaga
16. Sergio Agüero and Fernandinho
17. 10-0
18. Wolverhampton Wanderers
19. Leicester City (2021)
20. Bristol City

Round 12 - Other European Competitions

1. Champions League and Europe League winners
2. Chelsea
3. Liverpool
4. AC Milan and Barcelona
5. Stade Louis II
6. Atlético Madrid
7. Radamel Falcao
8. Windsor Park
9. 1999
10. Albania
11. Lazio
12. Alex Ferguson
13. Dynamo Kiev
14. Rangers
15. Villa Park
16. Nayim
17. 2021/22
18. 2008
19. Newcastle
20. Bodø/Glimt

Round 13 - British Isles League Football

1. Old Firm
2. Shamrock Rovers
3. Derry City
4. Scottish Professional Football League
5. 12
6. Cardiff Metropolitan University
7. Rangers
8. Aberdeen
9. Linfield and Glentoran
10. St. Patricks Athletic and Bohemians
11. 10
12. 1890
13. Queen's Park
14. Gretna
15. Easter Road
16. Kris Boyd
17. St Mirren
18. 12, Motherwell vs Hibernian, 6-6
19. The New Saints
20. Marc Lloyd Williams

Round 14 - Premier League II

1. Liverpool
2. Petr Čech
3. Ryan Giggs
4. Anfield
5. 2015/16
6. Matt Le Tissier
7. Jack Grealish
8. Turf Moor
9. Crystal Palace
10. 1999
11. Derby County, 11
12. Mo Salah, 32
13. Teddy Sheringham
14. Oldham
15. Sergio Agüero
16. Richard Dunne
17. Swindon Town
18. Emmanuel Adebayor
19. Ryan Giggs, 134 times
20. Brian Deane

Round 15 - La Liga II

1. Philippe Coutinho
2. Javier Tebas Medrano
3. Santander
4. Samuel Eto'o
5. Sevilla
6. Terry Venables
7. Camp Nou
8. Barcelona
9. 22
10. 1
11. 2002
12. 9
13. Hugo Sánchez
14. 50,000 (48,600)
15. Madrid
16. Johan Cruyff
17. Andoni Zubizarreta
18. 3
19. Osasuna
20. Florentino Pérez

Round 16 - Serie A II

1. Associazione Calcio (association football)
2. Christian Vieri
3. Sampdoria
4. 18
5. 2006
6. Marek Hamšík
7. Napoli
8. Palermo
9. Brescia
10. 3 times
11. 66
12. Fiorentina
13. Patrick Vieira and Zlatan Ibrahimović
14. 2010
15. Sassuolo
16. Salernitana
17. TIM
18. Romelu Lukaku
19. Juventus
20. San Paulo

Round 17 - Bundesliga II

1. Allianz Arena
2. Brown
3. £50k
4. 9
5. Hamburg
6. Altintop
7. Reece Oxford
8. Swiss
9. 09
10. Rasenballsport
11. 2.Bundesliga
12. Serge Gnabry
13. Hertha Berlin
14. 1860 Munich
15. Schalke 04
16. Lucas Hernandez
17. Freiburg
18. Hamburg & Werder Bremen
19. Arjen Robben
20. Greuther Fürth

Round 18 - Ligue 1 II

1. 4
2. Loïc Perrin
3. Pauleta
4. Ajaccio and Bastia
5. 2016/17
6. Lens
7. Nice
8. 1930s (1932)
9. Kasper Dolberg
10. Lyon, 71 seasons
11. 13
12. 9
13. Steve Mandanda
14. Clairefontaine
15. Marseille
16. Strasbourg
17. Etienne Green
18. Thierry Henry
19. 15,000 (16,360)
20. 1986

Round 19 - Champions League II

1. Champions League
2. Cristiano Ronaldo
3. Bob Paisley, Carlo Ancelotti and Zinedine Zidane
4. Wanda Metropolitano
5. Hampden Park
6. Zlatan Ibrahimović
7. Adidas
8. Malmö
9. 3
10. Tony Britten
11. Luiz Adriano
12. 2
13. Manchester United, 1998/99
14. Roy Makaay
15. Barcelona, 2007/08-2012/13
16. Nyon
17. 7
18. Marcel Desailly
19. Paolo Maldini
20. Karim Benzema

Round 20 - Wiki Game I
1. Ricardo Quaresma
2. Paul Gascoigne
3. Xavi Hernández
4. Stanley Matthews
5. Gabriel Batistuta
6. Mo Johnstone
7. Andrea Pirlo
8. Javier Zanetti
9. Diego Forlán
10. Ferenc Puskás
11. Johan Cruyff
12. John Charles
13. Thiago Silva
14. Fyodor Cherenkov
15. Mats Hummels
16. Diego Maradona
17. Landon Donovan
18. Lukas Podolski
19. Louis Saha
20. Mark González

Round 21 - Stadiums I
1. Athletic Bilbao - San Mames
2. Atlanta United - Mercedes-Benz Stadium
3. Atlético Madrid - Wanda Metropolitano
4. Basel - St. Jakob-Park
5. Colorado Rapids - Dicks Sporting Goods Park
6. Exeter City - St James Park
7. Fiorentina - Stadio Artemio Franchi
8. Iran - Azadi Stadium
9. Kaiserslautern - Fritz-Walter-Stadion
10. Marseille - Stade Velodrome
11. Newcastle United - St James' Park
12. Porto - Estádio do Dragão
13. Preston North End - Deepdale
14. River Plate - El Monumental
15. Sochi - Fisht Olympic Stadium
16. Stuttgart - Mercedes-Benz Arena
17. Udinese - Stadio Friuli
18. Villareal - El Madrigal
19. Wrexham - Racecourse Ground
20. Zenit St Petersburg - Krestovsky Stadium

Round 22 - World Cup
1. Brazil, Five
2. Uruguay
3. Sweden
4. Graham Poll
5. Mario Götze
6. Miroslav Klose
7. Mexico, 1986
8. Panama and Iceland
9. Pelé
10. Once (1966)
11. Mexico
12. Brad Friedel
13. Estadio Azteca
14. England
15. East Germany
16. Pickles
17. Italy
18. Austria 7-5 Switzerland
19. Argentina
20. Roger Milla

Round 23 - Euros
1. Soviet Union and Yugoslavia
2. 24
3. 1958
4. London
5. Germany/Spain, 3
6. Eder
7. Cristiano Ronaldo
8. Every 4 years
9. Henri Delaunay
10. Twice
11. Iker Casillas, 9
12. Otto Rehhagel
13. Antonín Panenka
14. Joachim Low
15. Michel Platini, 9
16. Fernando Torres
17. Chris Coleman
18. Netherlands and Belgium
19. Greece
20. Finland & North Macedonia

Round 24 - Copa America
1. 1916
2. Argentina/Uruguay, 15
3. Bolivia
4. 1
5. 2007
6. United States
7. True
8. Brazil
9. 10
10. Dog
11. Qatar
12. Brazil
13. Chile
14. Colombia
15. None
16. 7-0
17. Japan
18. Richarlison
19. Paolo Guerrero
20. Mexico

Round 25 - AFCON
1. African Cup of Nations
2. Senegal
3. 1957
4. Samuel Eto'o
5. None
6. Ivory Coast
7. Egypt
8. 44
9. 24
10. 3
11. Egypt
12. Ethiopia and Sudan
13. Hervé Renard
14. Sadio Mané
15. Hossam Hassan
16. Christopher Katongo
17. Emmanuel Mayuka
18. Tunisia
19. Angola
20. Claude Le Roy

Round 26 - CONCACAF Gold Cup
1. Every 2 years
2. Mexico
3. 16
4. 1991
5. Landon Donavan
6. 5-0
7. 7
8. FOX
9. Confederations Cup
10. US
11. Jamaica
12. South Africa
13. Zero
14. Canada
15. Giovanni Dos Santos
16. South Korea
17. Confederation of North, Central America and Caribbean Association Football
18. Costa Rica
19. Volkswagen
20. 1985

Round 27 - Asia Cup & OFC Nations Cup
1. Japan
2. 46
3. 24
4. 1954
5. Hong Kong
6. Cambodia
7. Saudi Arabia
8. Israel
9. Qatar
10. Zero
11. Ange Postecoglou
12. Keisuke Honda
13. Australia
14. Tahiti
15. Papua New Guinea
16. 1973
17. New Caledonia
18. Chris Wood
19. Tim Cahill
20. Chris Killen

Round 28 - World Cup II

1. Ossie Ardiles and Ricardo (Ricky) Villa
2. Geoff Hurst, 3, 1966
3. Cafu and Ronaldo
4. Pele, 10
5. Daniel Passarella
6. Peter Shilton, 10
7. Javier Mascherano
8. Italy
9. Brazil
10. 3.5 billion
11. Carlos Alberto
12. Oleg Salenko
13. Five
14. Germany
15. Mauro Camoranesi
16. Gabriel Batistuta
17. Lothar Matthäus
18. Maarten Stekelenburg
19. Benedikt Höwedes
20. Steven N'Zonzi

Round 29 - Stadiums II

1. Santiago Bernabéu
2. Stadio delle Alpi
3. Borussia Dortmund
4. Everton
5. Benfica
6. La Bombonera
7. Carrow Road
8. Highbury
9. 2007
10. Birmingham
11. North Korea
12. 99,000
13. California
14. Flamengo and Fluminese
15. Tottenham Hotspur Stadium
16. Ajax
17. Vicente Calderón
18. Johannesburg
19. 82,000
20. Luzhniki Stadium

Round 30 - Lionel Messi

1. Xavi
2. Getafe
3. 7
4. Adidas
5. Ten
6. Newell's Old Boys
7. Neymar and Luis Suarez
8. Andres
9. 5ft 7in (1.70m)
10. 4
11. A napkin
12. 22
13. 2008 Beijing
14. 'The Flea'
15. Arsenal
16. Rosario
17. 3
18. Italy
19. 1987
20. Catholic

Round 31 - Cristiano Ronaldo

1. 2003
2. Real Madrid
3. Nike
4. Sporting Lisbon
5. Edison Cavani
6. Five
7. Five
8. 9
9. Cristiano Jr
10. 6ft 1in (1.85m)
11. Funchal, Madeira
12. Dimitri Payet
13. 1985
14. £12m
15. Kaká
16. Raúl
17. Coca-Cola
18. Shakhtar Donetsk
19. Quarter-finals
20. Paulinho

Round 32 - England

1. Wayne Rooney
2. Wembley Stadium
3. Harry Kane
4. Peter Shilton
5. Croatia
6. Theo Walcott
7. Martin Peters
8. Billy Wright
9. Walter Winterbottom
10. Terry Venables
11. Scotland
12. 9
13. Michael Owen
14. Harry Maguire
15. Admiral
16. Blue
17. 27th
18. 13-0
19. Hungary
20. Denmark

Round 33 - Wiki Game II

1. Kevin Keegan
2. Charlie Hurley
3. Radamel Falcao
4. Brett Emerton
5. Franz Beckenbauer
6. Eusébio
7. Chris Wondolowski
8. Keisuke Honda
9. Juninho Pernambucano
10. Lev Yashin
11. Mustapha Hadji
12. Luís Figo
13. Hristo Stoichkov
14. Dwayne De Rosario
15. Hidetoshi Nakata
16. Billy Wright
17. Oleg Blokhin
18. Simão Sabrosa
19. Bobby Moore
20. Lothar Matthäus

Round 34 - Remember the Score?

1. Uruguay 2-1 Brazil
2. Barcelona 2-8 Bayern Munich
3. Liverpool 0-2 Arsenal
4. Portugal 5-3 North Korea
5. Australia 31-0 American Samoa
6. England 4-2 West Germany (AET)
7. Middlesbrough 8-1 Manchester City
8. Tottenham Hotspur 4-5 Arsenal
9. Monaco 8-3 Deportivo La Coruña
10. Italy 3-2 Brazil
11. Soviet Union 3-4 Belgium (AET)
12. Ajax 2-3 Tottenham Hotspur
13. Uruguay 1-1 Ghana (4-2 pens)
14. Real Madrid 7-3 Eintracht
15. Liverpool 5-4 Alavés (AET)
16. Tottenham Hotspur 6-4 Reading
17. Barcelona 6-1 Paris Saint Germain
18. West Bromwich Albion 5-5 Manchester United
19. Italy 4-3 West Germany (AET)
20. Barcelona 0-4 Dynamo Kiev

Round 35 - Women's Football

1. 1969
2. Alexia Putellas
3. Barclays
4. 2001
5. Lyon
6. Barcelona
7. Ellen White
8. Norwegian
9. USA
10. Hope Brown
11. Vivianne Miedema
12. 12
13. 2011
14. Marta
15. Lucy Bronze
16. Alex Morgan
17. Christine Sinclair
18. Emma Hayes
19. 354
20. Abby Wambach

Round 36 - Laws of the Game
1. Red
2. 17
3. 18 yards
4. 30 minutes
5. 90 meters
6. 120 meters
7. 4
8. 7
9. 5
10. 12 yards
11. 24ft x 8ft. (7.32 x 2.44m)
12. Video Assistant Referee
13. 10 yards
14. At least 5 feet
15. 400 grams
16. 15 minutes
17. 1965
18. Hawk-Eye
19. A goal in extra time that wins the match providing the teams aren't level at half-time in extra time.
20. Indirect free kick

Round 37 - 50/50
1. Celtic
2. Spurs
3. Wednesday (4 to 1)
4. Burnley (£15m to £9.9m)
5. Frank Lampard (177 to 175)
6. Joe Hart (75 to 73)
7. Arsène Wenger (828 to 810)
8. Eden Hazard (£103.5m to £90.9m)
9. Paolo Maldini (2011 to 2014)
10. Ian Wright (28 to 27)
11. Xavi (767 to 674)
12. Hungary (2 to 1)
13. Gabriel Batistuta (10 to 8)
14. Wales (8th to 13th)
15. Bayern Munich (5 to 2)
16. Steaua Bucureşti (1 to 0)
17. New York City (1 to 0)
18. São Paulo (3 to 1)
19. Alessandro Del Piero (24 to 2)
20. Liverpool (6 to 3)

You have now come to the end of the quiz. I really hope you have enjoyed the book and have learnt lots of awesome facts about the beautiful game to impress your mates and family.

As a small independent publisher, positive reviews left on our books go a long way to attracting new readers who share your passion for the game.

If you are able to take a few minutes out of your day to leave a review it would be greatly appreciated!

If you spot any issues you would like to raise please do **email me before leaving a negative review** with any comments you may have.

I will be more than happy to liaise with you and can offer refunds or updated copies if you are unhappy with your purchase.

kieran.brown2402@gmail.com

Printed in Great Britain
by Amazon

83897837R00054